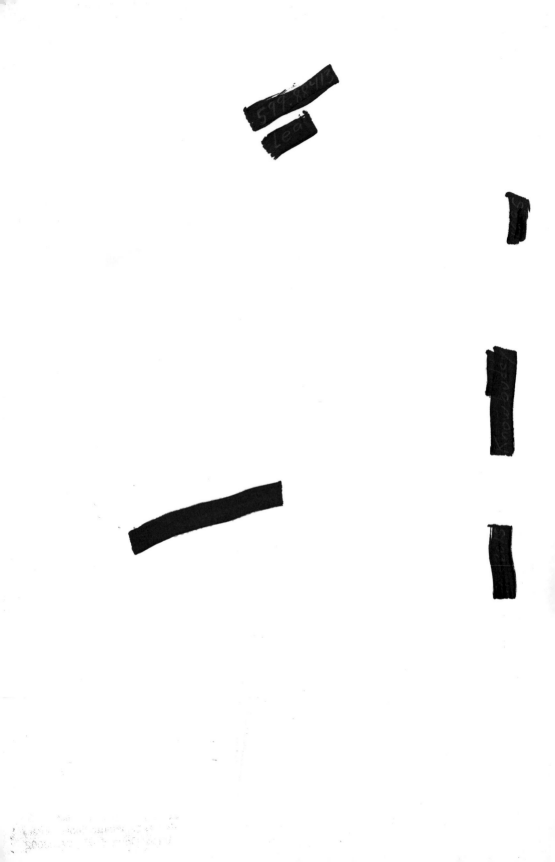

SUPER CUTE!

Baby Gorillas

by Christina Leaf

BELLWETHER MEDIA • MINNEAPOLIS, MN

Note to Librarians, Teachers, and Parents:

Blastoff! Readers are carefully developed by literacy experts and combine standards-based content with developmentally appropriate text.

Level 1 provides the most support through repetition of high-frequency words, light text, predictable sentence patterns, and strong visual support.

Level 2 offers early readers a bit more challenge through varied simple sentences, increased text load, and less repetition of high-frequency words.

Level 3 advances early-fluent readers toward fluency through increased text and concept load, less reliance on visuals, longer sentences, and more literary language.

Level 4 builds reading stamina by providing more text per page, increased use of punctuation, greater variation in sentence patterns, and increasingly challenging vocabulary.

Level 5 encourages children to move from "learning to read" to "reading to learn" by providing even more text, varied writing styles, and less familiar topics.

Whichever book is right for your reader, Blastoff! Readers are the perfect books to build confidence and encourage a love of reading that will last a lifetime!

This edition first published in 2015 by Bellwether Media, Inc.

No part of this publication may be reproduced in whole or in part without written permission of the publisher.
For information regarding permission, write to Bellwether Media, Inc., Attention: Permissions Department,
5357 Penn Avenue South, Minneapolis, MN 55419.

Library of Congress Cataloging-in-Publication Data

Leaf, Christina, author.
  Baby Gorillas / by Christina Leaf.
    pages cm. – (Blastoff! Readers. Super Cute!)
  Summary: "Developed by literacy experts for students in kindergarten through grade three, this book introduces baby
gorillas to young readers through leveled text and related photos."– Provided by publisher.
  Audience: Ages 5-8.
  Audience: K to grade 3.
  Includes bibliographical references and index.
  ISBN 978-1-62617-170-1 (hardcover : alk. paper)
  1. Gorilla–Infancy–Juvenile literature. I. Title. II. Series: Blastoff! Readers. 1, Super Cute!
  QL737.P94L428 2015
  599.88413′92–dc23
                        2014034761

Printed in the United States of America, North Mankato, MN.

Table of Contents

Gorilla Infant!

A baby gorilla is called an infant. It lives in a **troop**.

Getting Around

The **newborn** infant cannot walk. Mom carries her baby close to her chest.

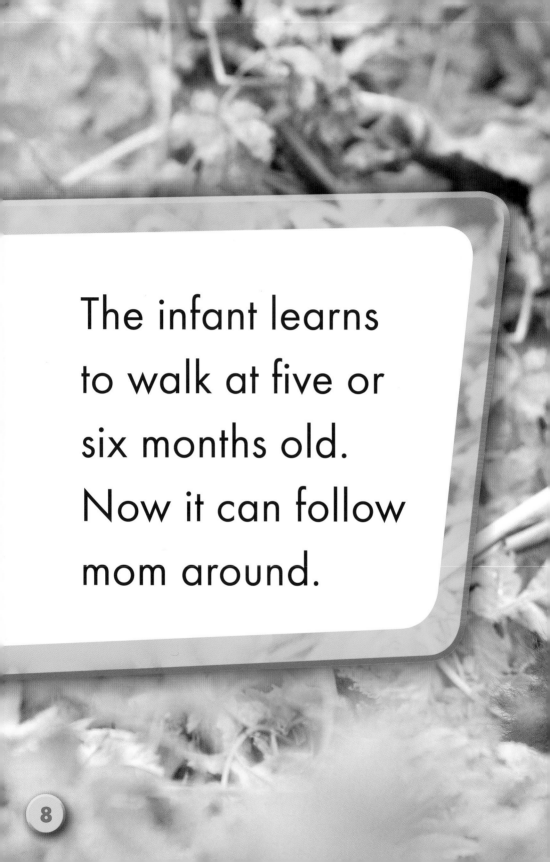

The infant learns to walk at five or six months old. Now it can follow mom around.

The baby loves piggyback rides. It is safe on mom's back.

An infant **nurses** for up to three years. Then it eats leaves, fruits, and bark.

The infant likes to explore. It climbs trees. Sometimes it swings on **vines**.

It makes friends
with other babies.
They like to
play-fight.

Then mom **grooms** her baby. This helps them **bond**.

At night, each adult gorilla makes a nest. The infant shares with mom. Snuggle time!

Glossary

bond—to grow close

grooms—cleans

newborn—just recently born

nurses—drinks mom's milk

troop—a group of gorillas that live together

vines—plants that twist up trees; some vines hang from tree branches.

To Learn More

AT THE LIBRARY

Faulconer, Maria. *A Mom for Umande.* New York, N.Y.: Dial Books for Young Readers, 2014.

Leaf, Christina. *Baby Orangutans.* Minneapolis, Minn.: Bellwether Media, 2015.

Zobel, Derek. *Gorillas.* Minneapolis, Minn.: Bellwether Media, 2012.

ON THE WEB

Learning more about gorillas is as easy as 1, 2, 3.

1. Go to www.factsurfer.com.

2. Enter "gorillas" into the search box.

3. Click the "Surf" button and you will see a list of related web sites.

With factsurfer.com, finding more information is just a click away.

Index

The images in this book are reproduced through the courtesy of: Jens Meyer/ Corbis, front cover, pp. 4-5;
Ronald Wittek/ agefotostock, pp. 6-7; Pilchards/ Alamy, pp. 8-9; Eric Gevaert, pp. 10-11; Roberto Cattini/
Sopa RF/ Corbis, pp. 12-13; Rolf Schulten/ Glow Images, pp. 14-15; Suzi Eszterhas/ Corbis, pp. 16-17,
18-19; KimballStock, pp. 20-21.